METROPOLE

Geoffrey G. O'Brien

# METROPOLE

University of California Press   Berkeley  Los Angeles  London

**NATIONAL ENDOWMENT FOR THE ARTS**

This project is supported in part by an award from the National Endowment for the Arts.

University of California Press, one of the most distinguished university presses in the United States, enriches lives around the world by advancing scholarship in the humanities, social sciences, and natural sciences. Its activities are supported by the UC Press Foundation and by philanthropic contributions from individuals and institutions. For more information, visit www.ucpress.edu.

University of California Press
Berkeley and Los Angeles, California

University of California Press, Ltd.
London, England

Library of Congress Cataloging-in-Publication Data

O'Brien, Geoffrey G. (Geoffrey Gordon), 1969–
    Metropole / Geoffrey G. O'Brien
        p.   cm. — (New California poetry ; 33)
    ISBN 978-0-520-26887-6 (pbk. : alk. paper)
    I. Title.
    PS3615 B75M47   2011
    811'.6—dc22                                     2010032587

Manufactured in the United States of America

20   19   18   17   16   15   14   13   12   11
10   9   8   7   6   5   4   3   2   1

The paper used in this publication meets the minimum requirements of ANSI/NISO Z39.48-1992 (R 1997) (*Permanence of Paper*).

# CONTENTS

METROPOLE

## VAGUE CADENCE

An away of practice the other is
Like a river out of acts the other is
Hapless, unheard, with marks upon him
Having dallied in tarrying unwisely
Backlit at an undecidable remove
In a house of marks the other is
Useless deciding whether to go
Or wait in best practices like a child
A hapless river filled with sand
For years it flows like unmarked rope
Years of saying as it moves away
Are the undecided water others bring
Like the child of acts the other is
Saying to himself the other is
A hapless river practicing its flow
A house that moves to where one was
With all years off the water goes
The lights are on so the dark is out
Like the useless children others are
A certain building dream within
A part of speech without a name

## BOHEMIAN GROVE

Grab our missing spears and begin
to think the Bohemian Grove, trees,
theatricals, songs that hold exquisite
filterings of sunlight down to the boys
were women there in the powerful glades,
in the 20s, there's nothing like it, to have
loins for the first time running around
in leaves, in the 70s I sang a song of we
became ourselves again as women, specifically
houris, the "leaves of love" falling
by chopper and could see the security cordon
of leaves running around excited to be
playing a part in the hush of the woods
Donald called me "songbird" and to be fit
for the world one must periodically leave it,
affectionately, for the age and straightness of trees
in the 80s, whispering at the clearing's edge
about how to keep both houses, no one hurt
when respect is earned by singing a short theme
in the 40s, at the tree line, theatricals, excited
to be putting on a helmet and running around
in the dark, on my knees in the sun
being told as a group what to do about
how soft I was, the pillows in my chamber
with choppers landing and a glow through the trees

spread uncomfortably around the clearing
till there's nothing like it, going missing
and the distance you begin to think, respect
hushing the woods with a part to play
blacked out in the secret authority
of choosing a heavy gold dress to wear
over on the other side of the clearing
songs hold the men like houris
for the first time leaving the world
affectionately at play in choppers and leaves
no one is hurt at the edge of themselves
running from the news of sunlight
into heavy dresses the warriors wore
for a production of the 50s, absence of birdsong
there in the powerful soil.

## POEM BEGINNING TO END

The trees are men, men strange,
Strangers come into a house to speak
Across a table made of trees.
Waking was fighting at it while
Looking at a thing you own is
Sleeping outdoors without knowing why
The reasons escape, so continuing
To eat and drink. I think you have to

In order to be ready, a cup seriously
Open, ready to talk or gesture with it,
Show the house has no roof,
Men are coming in, this is a cup.
We make a tableau called embarrassment
At a physical past, the one prepared
Accordingly your instincts stopped
Now in admitting daylight

I was fighting or talking about this
Feeling taken from a box of scarves,
Cardboard box from another move
Marked by faint incursions, games
So called because all was still
In play, that table for instance,
Where a hand is trained to follow
The eye into goals, this cup

Moving on its own through the single
Family dwelling space contracts to,
Angry from the outset
That a hand is still involved
And scene. I went back to sleep
In the middle of our argument,
Speech about forgotten labor
A lamp can sing with its head bent

Remarks I should anticipate I am
The shadow objections to, streaming
Out from the faucet to be cut in half
By hand. The entire room far off
Talk content to happen tone
On tone, the strong illusion,
And night, deaf as a mural,
Not made so much as lovingly

Assembled from memories of those
Who couldn't get out of the way,
Now here in the form of a cup
Alien when brought to bed
From table and the table not
Made so much as overturned,
Evolving from its legs a depth
Morning is the answer to

## LEFT BEHIND

To speak of autumn reasonably
As knowing tasks remain undone
I forgot the password "autumn"
Moving through the empty lots
Gray gates deserving paint
Fewer cars on the road, to speak
Of these cars I forgot autumn had
Come wasting its credibility
There was a gray to repaint
Those rituals for keeping spring
From happening, I was trying to
Be evenhanded about why fall
Held in fidelity to everything is
How absentminded lyrics put it
Written that way while cars
Passed modestly, run-on
Sentences beginning "I can't"
Recall all the things that go here
Lots empty or not yet
Doing the holiday errands
Would be one way to phrase
A low point autumn deserves
Credit for or driving towards
Becomes the shop I forget
To stop sensibly at autumn

As in lots of things to do
Modesty forbids me to mention
There is a gray gate in lyric
Before getting on the road again
I'd say autumn is only to be
Pointed at if willing to waste
The rest of the day in driving
Embarrassed to have said it

## POEM WITH NO GOOD LINES

Without its being entirely true
Which will thrive is a matter of opinion
I love you in an ordinary way
The sea sits between all the lands

They can't hear it for what it is
I recall this at inopportune times
One of the hours reserved for just that
Way to keep great things unsaid

It runs down my arm and into my hand
I can't wait till you get here next week
Otherwise why give it to us
And were told to go back inside

He'll never admit that in person
Little blue flowers, not many or long
They look pretty uncomfortable
Earlier and earlier, or so it seems

The red shirt of being without
Twisting smell of pineapple sage
Just a few episodes left
I thought I heard them coming in

I could be more generous with my time
My friend's life will take him away
Each thing that distracts me at night
It turns out they're more of a cult

First camera's shutter then saw or alarm
You still haven't told me how it went
We'll be more careful with the lights
A softness clear around the eye

His success bothers me much more than yours
The way the onion glides through the ground
They obstruct the view and feel okay
Whatever I might have said at the time

Some have black bodies and gold breasts
If in the same room I couldn't help myself
I stood there while they spoke to the boys
One of the reasons they'll be back I'm sure

The vitality of youth is irreplaceable
That bird makes a brave chipping sound
It's too painful to watch them play
Within a makeshift university

To recover a portion of what I then had
Confusing jasmine and mock orange
Acceptable levels of anger and shame
A list of only yellow things

I wish you'd been able to stay the week
Like trying to describe the sky at night
It's only going to get worse and worse
I'm happy about it if you are

He went back to the job again
The moss grows on one side of the trees
It loses its heat as it cooks down
Without a pen I can't explain

The stupid lichen of getting up late
His way of stumbling through a speech
It will continue to get worse I'm sure
I should do at least what I said I would

May 1st is followed by May 2nd
Attacking its mirror image with zeal
I think of those I love to know
Which is so far the cost of it

He really has a chance to now
I stood there while they talked to them
It's useless but I'd leap on him
Attracted by the sound of running water

Break-ins are common where neighborhoods meet
Her shoulder blades and the small of her back
I don't participate and they don't like that
Watching them run through the terminal

Every morning I check how I feel
They take turns guarding it
There are really no good options
It will all start again so soon

Each season moves to a new focus
He asked why I think of audience that way
I'm going to tell you other people's dreams
The silver band as it snakes through rock

At any time conjuring the deaths that occur
It gets easier to speak to them
I tested all things, but a few were long-lived and at large
I realize now they can't be separated

There's almost no good way to do this
He's pure figurehead and yet I would
They call just about every night
A reddish head and light brown breast

Not until everyone can and not even then
You've got to respect how fast mint grows
It sounds like a bomb but it can't be
I just want more for your life

My friends are the writers I happen to know
Cloud shadows on foothills while aloft
Don't open the window or she'll get out
To do it in days

The pink hearse of drinking too much
No locks will deter them for long
I'll tell you what woke me this time
The hole in sexual love

Their delicate dusty bodies are alert
The ruins all lit up at night
I just can't seem to call them back
At least ten minutes every day

Encroachments of ivy across the back wall
There should be ample time for that
I'm thinking instead of a heteronym
Imagine my relief it's not what you meant

Focus as a form of enraged sympathy
That's the kind of company he keeps
In the taverna of virtual experience
A crapshoot whether it fruits this year

To go on too long as though under way
Still bodies in liquid on shelves in locked rooms
The net of interest recloses each night
Never yet photographed during courtship

Then she quoted Hebrews 13.3
Genre to which the rest are invited
I'll go where you go even if I don't come
A smart time to move far inland

I probably would if in the same room
Her neck in profile and the top of the head
The most fluent and honest I've felt in a year
Let's hope he'll choose more wisely now

# FAILED CATALOG

So only a series of approved rivalries,
Color struggles in distant cities
Appearing white or yellow then
White again in new locales,
Initial contact between parties
In anticipation of a use: tulips

For their easy display of chambers
But not the jonquil's distracted bell
Looking off a modest progress.
Lantana for its safer forms but no
Schadenfreude of the trumpet vine
Laughing at a year's pastel debris.

So only a series of approved devices,
Slashes that curve until coils yield
White rose, yellow rose, moss rose, etc.
The eyes of dresses walking by, stopped
By a scene their stopping closes
To any further investment. But now

Even red fills the victory garden
With ill-advised exaltations, planned
Surprise of a world become all
Nervousness, demanding proof
Come back. It likes things to
Arrive by unnoticeable kinds of mail

Red can count itself quietly
Among, nothing more than
An aged person in a playground
Thinking of secluded industries, what
Goes on elsewhere making it through
In tame flashes, dream of hearing

Laughs from a set of relations
Easy to turn down. I like to think
Laughter is first yellow then red
As the damage spreads to the rest,
Child in bright shirt, bodiless,
Detainable only in the dwarf form

Of mountain laurel as it grows without support.
There are several other things to say,
Some of which extend beyond the page,
So any upward motion half intended,
Limited battles materials begin,
All the citizens in any of their things,

How the furniture ends up on the street
In a dream there's no sequel to
Picking out one thing at another's
Expense, and living here not there
Where the rose is ticking. All clocks
Bombs to the sweet pea which still

Must think its way in bunched tasks
Beyond the sin of overhaste. The name
Trails behind on a small stake
Brought forward each inaudible spring
To a correspondence. I like to think
Hello is a way of saying it's vast

Even local colors are capable of,
Haziness of sun first yellow gauze
Then madder, maize, war, etc.

## FORMS OF BATTLE

Something about the open fate
All ills flower from, smoke and rain
You can shoot the future through
Reminds me of a fallen sound
Less song than circular hum
Defining the monotony of acts
Soldiering on half a world away
If sound had a face it would be
Blown apart immediately
There would be many things
About it left over to flower
Almost an infinite veil by now
I had a friend who heard things in it
Sole protection against dangers
And so I made my way across
The facial terrain to be with her
Balancing the head atop its act
Of white noise both fun and ugly
But there we were, walking the trail
Designed to reverse bad thoughts
By crossing itself at several points
Unclear anything happened after
Except the way we composed
A stay thrown back against the room
Lights ashamed to be on and on

Nothing left but the bitter verbs
Of manner of motion away from a source
The pastoral jail of refrain
And so I put my head under her arm
As though to leave America

## THREE YEARS

Toying with a gun as a train goes past
June is what I'd imagined, dark
intermittent woods set off
by the whiteness of a collar, a book
I can't believe we're left alone with.
The woods still there, dark woods,
a system of humble requests. Each takes
a day to appear among strangers,
laughs at motion and sleep then fades
through the camouflage of features
coming back for an August now
still dust and low phrases. Simply
by doing my tragic morning hygiene
I read the book: slept, washed, awoke,
washed, slept in what might be
a training ring but isn't and then.
The compulsion to chase rain, repeat
a sheer survival, books by friends,
how you enter the street with a smile
more warped ornament than bas-relief,
give an opaque lecture on a portrait
one doesn't know the laws of. November:
I read aloud some traveling conclusions
December must praise and die. Years

pass through the common instants.
Other pursuits I've put aside but how
I refuse to leave remains in gray force,
they won't come for me and I go to them
a little at a time. And today massing
like a wet green hill, individual, huge.
For the steep part of the afternoon I was
away from it then acted. You, I said
and gave a little shove. January. You,
I allowed, who is neither external nor internal,
written down a few days ago by tourists.
Every day I wanted to get out of bed
but the nature of its horizon forms
a length and width defeating emendation
and I stay there for a long time wanting
to tell anyone about the close call. February:
my life for the click of a moment
far from me, tragic shirt hung up
in an old hall attacked by applause.
March, the artist at risk, ironwork, stories
about May. I learned of it only afterwards
when it was again in the future, began
to talk about it constantly—March, I said,
really believing it was more than measurement.

I leaned my face into its basin and emerged
clean, ready for work and for a language
in which speaking is a single letter.
Otherwise why this whole time have I?
And today is your birthday but instead
of spending it with you I'm hurtling
through crypts, not even the time that's over,
celebrating with the private exertions
April barely tolerates. I in turn treat it
like a poor parent, living just inside
acquaintances I'd better leave, hours
chained to benches since late morning,
the adjoining room rushing past,
a tunnel blithely repeating the day
before the day before yesterday, habits.
More is suspect, only ideas. I fall, I fell,
conjugation on the underground platform
restless and vicious towards evening. It seems
like enough if shared on a bough but only if.
I wash my hands carefully in advance
and stare down at the tracks of contact,
waiting for little events, the other night
at the table: first appearance of August
in conversation, ghostlike. I know this heat

has a purpose other than to move us around
but it's only these rhythms that are felt
rather than the estate itself. Wrote yesterday
evening and the day before yesterday
but no knock on the door resulted. Yesterday
wrote in praise of orderly flows but not
yesterday evening, which was spent waiting.
Yawned while alone to indicate a hollow body
admitting of exchanges. This directive
to rip up private records for the public good
makes the days bunch up and September
knows this, though by September I mean
those collected there to keep spring
from happening. But it did, at least once
rising out to the entire child of atmosphere,
invited to read that face for its cues. October,
dust on the base of a shelf. I finish nothing
because unwatched. I walked around alone
in a breath, its factory, probably sick
or at least uselessly accompanied on.
More examples of the way a city confers
smoothness of strolling for three hours
onto recollected surfaces then removes it.
October, a carousel of quarrels unperformed,

very little room for the actors. Or only time
to console myself with descriptions of the spin.
At six o'clock I met the age, the mother-work,
merry and dead; at other times it was equally present
without the sense of an encounter dominating.
Possibly neither of us noticed that today
I stood all afternoon expanding like grain,
crying from the single eye of my mouth
while in contemplation of hidden spaces.
Again I feel late summer's disowned me
and left me unprepared for plain dealing;
each morning when I rise I splash water
on temple and pulse and begin a second
ritual awakening behind the stage
so narrow your spirits gain entry after.
I had a similar feeling once when digging,
not sure whether guest or employee
but working hard in a space shaped like winter
months; it turns me—this craving I have,
despite the fact it's common, to wake up
and see if I'm already gone, forget last night
by the afternoon and mumble deft sounds
of departure: November. In the newspapers,
in the wet sand of conversation, in the office,

in order to prove everything. November's habit
of repeating what I like about death,
an association of yesterday with trembling,
the slowness I felt that evening when of it.
Tuesday all day a continued farewell
no one notices, the lawyer's dream where I try,
gradually, to group everything in November
but it's shelved in the day before yesterday
so there's no chance, the effort wasn't mine
to make and now goes general, joining up
with a cold autumn morning suspiciously
full of before falling asleep. Now I'll try a sketch
for only the most humble of introductions
to November: already a sense everything
I conceived before falling asleep rides back.
Nor is November without its own dream:
I and this evening filled with mutual respect.
Does this make me one who is learning
the honesty of evil thoughts? Yesterday
the odor of having intended nothing
for three days fell from neck and arms.
I drew the blanket tighter to become
a hill myself, jealous of speech but unfit for it.
Thinking to read for once before going under

felt again on my body the weight of December
but why decide to record this fact when
I haven't thought anything else for five days.
Wednesday: a walk, another, beautiful lonely
tracking through the coming into being of
a beaded atmosphere like harmless diamonds,
survivable. Now I miss the slight spell I had
from them though its dissipation allows
me to speak, the same sweetness by which one
patiently submits to a book of street scenes
or will, past fatigue, sleep without climax.
Often I begin to climb the inward stair
because reading carved a doorway in the morning,
the old tricks roll by, spectacular lessons
from a disorganized education mostly spent
looking out windows' wide yields
with the desire to undergo more of it,
that sense of a large arch I had an image of
before falling asleep in the park. This is one
from a handful of images, periods of transition
that didn't belong to me exactly, more like
the past of my thoughts when it moves again,
a cold never of use to me at the time although
it turns out I've been quite productive. December:

a bad play about envy I don't feel the pains of,
my good periods don't have time to.
The body arrives and speaks its surface curl.
When I get into this habit for too long
my head is the wish of a diary filled
with mist, evening before it was anxious.
Then I arrive at this morning and I'm the bride
I keep waiting; no one will blame me if I say
only what I say. Then just a dateless morning,
half what I understand a character sketch
I run and press my face against, the other
a list of things that are easy to imagine
but unpleasant to hear: December,
an unfortunate man who is my feeling
while taking a walk, those lively passages
through alleys that return at will, bringing now
the urge to imitate nothing, run it through.
I felt fresh but sometimes I think this
was a planned effect, chosen I confess
carelessly from those still available.
December: the sudden turn in autobiography
one can't avoid. And it's only because
of how my vanity sluggishly interacts with dusk
I even noticed it form. What looks like a vise or mill

January and its silent products, each
destined for the large room supposed to be there,
the loud talking in the room. So passes
my rainy, quiet Sunday, I sit inert in the chair
describing a storm at sea, pose nude for the relatives.
The following evening is the back of silence:
drew nothing into consultation, thought only of
lamps, low tables, how they'd look at sea,
the ocean in summer, a bobbing otherness,
and how the currents would redeposit them
in the room from which they'd drifted.
Three days ago wrote a short tactful letter
permeating every part with years, coolness,
quiet conversation, evening walks,
a Monday convinced of its internal variety.
None of this was evident or returned.
I still have this letter in case I need to check
the changes already made, a task stored
just between not having and needing
a stabilizing force among the people going home.
February is then a joke I like to tell myself
in the small hours. I opened the front door to see
and yes, the melancholy was posing as row houses
but you can almost hear it. March

was apparently some old notebooks, a chain.
This the way I get tossed, so deserted by myself,
by everything endurable, that today always
seems to be moving day. Another time
I recite this without the slightest sign of belief,
it's an attitude I caught, a metaphor
enjoying its vogue, a compulsion of which
only the overcoat remains. Everything else
is sheer encouragement. I stumble out
into weeks on end of the necessity
of speaking my almost accepted effect.
Today painfully tired, spent if you like,
because I burned the last few days doing
the morning in strict sun, controlled sound
of a rug being swept in the next room.
Not to overestimate my focus but I can't
say what day now rules. Only that on the street
false impressions for the first time
in a week, a week still standing for a stretch
of unimaginable time that is had and lost.
How a winter day passes: in the morning
complete knowledge of desire for birdsong
breaking into how unevenly I hold forth
because I too can hear it. The rest of the day

is like May, the May of winter, being for
the first time in a while with extended family.
But yesterday cold weather divided out
in branches to horizon and I caught nothing,
nearly nothing, two letters without weight,
a stare that could merely follow rather
than direct, and met with much too little
resistance on the train, almost certainly a trick.
Saw nothing today. Tomorrow might begin a little,
modestly. Nothing for so long though. March 16.
Possessed, finally, by a little eddy of spring, wrote
that I upset night. Wrote nothing else but that
though in different words, words anyone could use
without knowing they now meant this. The next
morning's coffee, empty and large,
was unmistakably involved. If I arrive often
at this conclusion it's because that's the picture
of dissatisfaction presented by a street. Or so
I'd like to think because of how it relieves me
of much in the way of major responsibilities.
Say it enough times and it's August, admitted
as a hovering shape somewhere between
counselor and friend. It will be hard to rouse me
and yet I am the mirror shaken and exalted.

This whole month of spirited misdeliveries
no one noticed the cut of its coat, a heat
that is the layering of abandoned goals.
With so little to do I reconcile the morning
with the spent evening of the day before.
I put one day in the place of another and laugh
at how easy it is to become their secret arbiter.
A laugh that is not pain but has no claim
on pleasure either, a simple administration
involving hand, eye, and throat. A dream:
I find myself at "our house," a work of genius
and I the spectator with regular habits. A dream:
February arrives midsummer as a stray
thought and then walks out, the story
interrupted, the performance met with uncertainty.
I unbutton my vest to show the way behind is struck.
The image of early morning streets empties
from the set and yet I walk not to fill them
but because of an inner frontier I suffer from
all sides like a cold spring morning in June.
About five o'clock the wish for unthinking
solitude, for the day before yesterday, honey
of that picture. I stayed with it, what's left
out of a broadening and heightening

when the calendar fills: band of little golden
beads around tanned throat. July 19—
another gap like a bed sent effortless: so all
the inner tensing was for this, large statue
of a woman or man, days of it that defile
through the frosted ground-floor window,
small summary of arguments for and against
late July itself. Lengthening days in which
one is that extremity, at night a boat in a bay
of surprise. Now and then while trying to sleep
getting sick of waiting for it, permission to
drop down out of preparation for the news
of any war, all speaking a standing in
doorways, punishment for the happiness
of remaining in bed towards morning. Maybe
I've caught hold of myself, as though August
had an end. With clumsy, jerky movements,
perhaps I go sit in the corner of the house,
locked up voluntarily, but I don't forget it.
While I sit there in yesterday's favorite chair
October flows over the scratched windowsill
with a sudden confidence it won't appear again,
but this is a special pleasure like ignorance
returned to the few enforcing it, and I

intentionally slink through those real dreams
of streets where uncertainty moves like a clock.
One problem is that the toll perfects its citizens
even though that sound marks the line
where they meet without feeling. Another's
what are bells still doing here.
I think this alone in a den of humility,
entreaties almost, also the debris left behind
when an impossible residence changes hands.
I take the July–November train but get off
long before my stop is first announced.
November dream: to walk like a feeling would
and then become the fear of finding it
whitely merging in a corner of a store,
the evening before last becoming huge.
All dreams are like aimlessly escorting letters
to the country without any curiosity.
Which is to say, all dreams are like the last
Monday of the month, one at a time but full.
No push is really needed, only a fall
into a freshness altered by filled pages.
There are more people than ever and the days
laugh at them until they almost hear it.
December 31, streets especially half-concealed

by mist, the trains cancelled, poor sightlines.
It's no different a form of waiting than bright
sunshine denting the harbor would be
but that's to transform material sensations
and impoverish them in the process, as this
night is already doing. I should note that
somewhere where conductors would feel it.
I will: it's late December, I know this by
the bareness of my inappropriate arms
and entire continents of fatality, white snow's
potential to become a glowing blue
both hilarious and mercantile. I go to sleep
as the dusting of eaves and also meaning
to take the front door off its hinges, this
how I greet the shyer parts of the year.
Thursday and Friday are enough the same
I remember the game of features again.

## THE OTHER ARTS

I laughed at how the donor was
Ben preferred the laborers at rest
It was managed prospects of a day
Pouring in through concrete and glass
To make a second museum appear
The young girl caught between them
Painted silent under linden trees
I talked about the wheat and clothes
Designed to shield workers from sun
He said all style was still to be found
In the subject's dominant hand or ear
In tall white rooms a people moved
To their sense of a frozen music
Without details they moved then paused
To take a picture with their phones
Flowing in self-guided tours
Stopping as much to listen as stare
At said things if things could be said
The frequency of donkey and cow
Crowding in to get a look
Donor and victim still at their prayers
Rhythm's embarrassment appears on their face
As silent apology for moving at all
Like liquid stone the face still moves
In and out of famous colonnades

Where I laughed and was responded to
With remarks on impossible perspective
All the life in some of the folds
Which is like thinking everything is
Foreground of a background
The expense of the materials
Shining forth from three key places
On a diagonal barely visible
In the unsustained lines of her cloak
He observed of clouds they represent
What else could have happened
In half-worked fields the painting is

# WHITE OF THE EYES

That there are synonyms for things

Winter spring if at a distance

And that these things can be sold

Earbuds, track lights, cable, tones

That the joy of bad times is

Equivalent words, those set up

To make a chain into clouds

As many as let moments through

As many moments as there are

Shaking in the calendar

That seasons bring equivalent joys

The things to be sold in the stores

Cloud and cloud-shadow

More words for things than things

More the night inside them

Than one set up outside

That the pleasure of bad times is

To hear chain in change

See thing in night when it comes

Rearranged as cloud then clouds

That one, linked by time to those

While these others seem to hold

The joy of bad times equivalent

To a pleasure fallen as things

Like definitions at a distance

Winter follows if it does

## FOLIE À DEUX

For me it's a combination of things,
feeling a bit late, unproductive,
you see a lot of that, running
then following, whatever it is
they do when put in situations
and given one thing that sprouts
the horns of a general wound.
I don't have it, but there it is,
we're supposed to and I don't,
or even know what it means
given the fluid event, so I feel
it's a combination of things,
essentially all of them, gone.
I see it often, from a good ways off,
not realizing it but there it is
like a special body of armed men
over the horizon, multiplying,
and for much of the weekend
it's like this, sluggish, intimate
phrases that authorize night
so that even if it's over I'm happy
with the desire to pursue it again,

a kind of slashed leaf or wheel
added to the litany,
one of those things you start off
without and over the week restore.

# AMBIEN

My wish to be picked up
Still indistinct from lying down
Can't be disclosed or acted on
Much like the greens we're trained to see
Repeated actions over time
Become the season's passive voice
Neutral as grass and like it all seams
The average of their sentences
Requires building beds each night
His syntax fired but he didn't move
So much as bring the mattress to the street
And that was it, it lay there
At the end of March transmitting
Final sentences, the uses still
We're trained to see sun throw
On any common household thing
A glow the bed thrown out retains
A past implied persistently
By indentations in its shape
Even the first night of April
Will not dispel, mistakenly
Suggesting that the streets were men
Their flowing profile over time
With all the little folds intact
Durant and Geary, public paths

Intended motion answers to
All the ways an oak can be
In its most demanding season
Sudden deaths now known to cause
May, old bills spread out unpaid
Private rooms that move around
With no real application

Recently I learned the pleasures of narrative tasks, doing what they say, rotation of the image through a cloud. And coming back from this, a term after use, the house in pink lasts of sun. I learned to appeal and extract, the power of so doing, and also to give old equations and sighs. That was it mostly, a tour of the haze, and the rest lost in transit. Except the image—that I kept, looking somewhat ragged. Still a face though one a bit derived.

I put this device between mine and the rest and blew through it electronically. I was the spirit of oil in the desert, was told this all night, falling past the tasks of my friends. I rotated and shone, shone and spun, the gold in an eagle's mouth. I saw the sky as a set of zones, equally open, transited by opportunities. I told the story of its sigh as a ragged face would tell it, bitten and deserted. I asked the head to utter pink mist.

And come back to its house, and come back with a something having happened, run through a set of appealing transitions. The oil of the eagle dripped from my mouth as prophecy, flowing. The car burned, earth flew, but really I derived no pleasure. Letter not spirit, it was a narrative mainly of extracts, of losing bits of friends.

Still the sky spun through its zones, the face retained power till night, when it shone lost. I kept to my tasks: transparent prison, invented house, back and forth between them. Narrative an equation, poetry the power of doing countless things in the open, transited by the rest. At night the earth is an image of poetry but equally so is the flowing face, ragged and blown. Recently it is also the eagle, perhaps behind cloud.

To imprison that power and give it away, this is the mouth's pink task: spin gold into friends, friends into wells, use the well up. Of the tours that begin at night, the bird's ragged laughter, it would take too long to tell. And of the spirit of invention all I can give is this last extract, in which the mouth divides and blows a bit, saying nearly what it does.

## ECSTATIC NORM

The early autumn vacancies
Are a myth, are sometimes true
Remind me of something that is
Have just become near-valid
If my calculations are right
By what right do I speak of them
Beyond this vague sense I have
That such things are, are on
The verge, must refer to actions
Experienced, decisions undertaken
These buildings somewhat hollowed out
In accordance with easy decrees
As lovers ply a falling trade
Without approval or release
Buildings that, timed to appear, appear
Next to each other and hollow
It's a rumor howsoever solid
That time of year when clashes soften
And colors personify, nervous
Certain trees suggest themselves
As mollifying fountains in a storm
Supposedly soon taking place
Curious acid of the planted forms
Incursions that follow or surround

Visits you never hear about
Is it possible these are items in a list
Ways to enter every guild
The story of how a case is built

## HAVING SINCE MOVED ON

I tend to look across a chain
of things as lost complaints
whose taking place is its translation
made up and sealed off. I tend
to pour oil on all my possessions
to see what they then are,
half brought and partly taken,
peaks behind a sheen.
Exhausted after this, ready
to return from that place
and its demands, unconcerned
with the distant thing
still on this side, nevertheless
like a suggestion of perfume
I follow out its tendency
to where some chains begin.

## RESTRICTED PALETTE

You sleep as though dropped out of speech
and trusting that they won't come in,
it's you who's out invading houses,
looking for an older precedent because
this can't be right, the guns at the airport
no longer surprise, it feels familiar like
minor accidents repeatedly convened.
Starting out as a little patch that blends
into almost all surrounds the morning
asks so much of you: to tell things
as though they occurred, travel in lines
from a face to a lens. The days obeyed
like flashing lights, positions held give way
to waking harshly, impatient to
show new skill in retrieving names, each
perfect gold if it applies and declining to
the same song over and over again
you sleep through it, thinking the rigor
of a yellow still half-parted from
belongings, falling up the wall as sun
or copper pipes and brass fittings,
whatever spreads through the grid. You
move away from these ochreous features,
losing bonds to them the way the cabs
ignore the traffic lights, not yet ready

to venture out from no particular
place across a little sand of rights
you'd call morning if not half asleep.
I tell you these things while sure I can't.
I apply from within their painted lanes.
You wake only afterwards as though
on days protected from musical speech.

# THE SÜTTERLIN METHOD

October, that idiomatic dream
of flowers withdrawn from boxes,
the difficult herbarium
identical with an induced look
that should, during transfer, become
sketches of rows, morning blinds,
the bright black canal exerting force,
house and surroundings lazy or impaired
but does not. The colors regroup
in a box denied to the senses,
a dismal box that reminds me of
nothing other than the time
after bad plans are drawn, October
withdrawing along its beam,
delicate, harmless, that October
which belongs in a mutilated house
but doesn't remain there, hysterical,
yanked back through fresh ends
along the street-dream, the canal,
falling absurd into series of months
stubbornly former, the affair
come forward with a twinge
of access again to be denied,
means that should function
with some agility, push the air

from the corner of an eye
but do not. A botanical dream
of series whose ends are perceived
with alarm, patient, irrational,
small letters folded back in
to the slant of the other months
with a degree of unexpectedness
that should, if continued, but does not
continue, falling, layered, induced
months ago to do this, hold,
go out along a look that leaves
the senses, that could hang on
to wrongs while it spreads but,
the streaming core unproctored,
doesn't, the days resembling changes
made to an unmarked case, months
eddies in the water near a house,
water bright black clear glass
gone trackless as October, linked
to an area, hysterical, not there
to be sketched, unless and until
passing easily through the fray.

## DIZZY PROCESSION

The apprentices paint themselves how odd
The first line of a poem about painting
Would also be an unused rope
Designed to fray at both ends
Falling back among the rest
Odd the line would write itself out
In apprenticeship to others, agree
To matter as the poem frayed
Until the rope becomes a brush
I experience as waiting in lines
Full of the dryness of instruments
Predictable the rope frays where
You begin to hear a master speak
The first line of a finished style

## STREET CRY

As if the old game were playing again
a dream in which the rich are friendly
up to a point, a figure certain to be
met now merges with the one already
standing by the bed at night or made
of numbers in a complicated way
you shout half rising to meet it
before it disappears, given there
to understand the processes
the smile of a wealthy man is made
of, hidden work along the line,
he's come to explain why all
shouts are the shouts of children
in daylight form, the day game
that rains down on short notice,
permitted to go on like apples
neither frightening nor free they hang
over the bed without much choice
and I'm angry about trying to sleep

like a hill is still a hill and night
a temporary thing you hear
a shout you have made yourself
in order to wake up because
we'll have to pull together now

in the best of the wrong places
he seems to be hanging over you
cutting the fruit before it ripens,
talking from the podium about
values day puts a boot through
a window waking up remembers
to rise slowly out of options
receding in rows, smiling if not
that happy about mentioning
anything sends it dreamily out
the nearest of the institution's
gates, where we gather to be held
back, what happens afterward is
night, relatedness of much too little

light left on like nothing to be done,
that decision was made a year ago
today, in the middle of a cloudy phase
lasting longer than it's true when asleep
I see the body as a gun not yet
pointed at anything worth mentioning,
somewhat underused like orchards
you tend not to smile as much these days
with autumn in its magazines
there are many people under you

and to the endless side, shouting
apples in the rain, that kind
of game where you forgot about it
by the time the leisure crested
I was somewhat sad to be this
grass cut into sheets at night,
comfortable sleeping down a screen
glowing while he made the future private
money with no numbers on it

## TO BE READ IN EITHER DIRECTION

Certain fights I have with myself
Certain fights that resemble "dawn"
Preaching a weight at the corners of the eyes
And lights, lights like useless sympathy
A bed on top of another bed
Like a cloth torn free in
A certain struggle one might have

Inaudibly, technologies lament their falling into parts have scattered anywhere a world extends. I'm thinking of the loneliness of wheels, word processors conserving single lines in short-term memory. They have a second life in prison time moves slowly in the middle of their sentences. Both coasts remain themselves in crumbling but the phone just lies there, grounded planes. You'd need a failing light to understand this sense a form preceded me by several seconds passed without my noticing. Everything to date has been

Outside the bedroom buses stuffed with passengers pose family unawares. Pedestrians, commuters, worries pleased they're happening, equivalent designs. The square completely filled then drained, a battle neither can afford to win. And banners, nightsticks, chanting, things with arms—from over either shoulder daylight knows the march as angry signs but crowds at night are demonstrations minus signs (portfolios). A struggle: fighting with an absent force. The rally's unknown number when divided by itself

Part ear, part gun, each eye records its own reports. The lights go off in all the subway cars they won't come back they're on now. Temporary darkness: where travelers feel young in touching strangers unpredictably. A swinging motion justifies brief introductions, speech unshared. The Hudson dredging projects left the water flowing cleaner than the 70s supplied a model for our future rationing: a synonym for anagrams, for staying with a split describing things will never have

The sounds of other worlds the sirens promise going by. France was Gaul but not for those who met invading waves. And platforms passed at speed, their standing motionless in honor of an underpainting, residues of plans. I haven't learned the word for serial tableaus, points along forgetful lines, will use experience till then, by which I mean coruscant lights in tunnels bent on doing prior plans. The speed at which they tell you damage reigns becomes attractive pace. A fantasy: fast-forwarding surveillance tapes

How office buildings suck their workers in—equipped, alive, whatever— syllables within a language made of phrases; any anger mostly sympathetic dancing while asleep. The dial tone also mad, a rage at waiting made specific song. Command prompts with their silent rhythm come to mind as well. Inmates, adolescents running through construction sites at night, the soldiers of another thing entirely. The proper subject chases new experience the rest will follow suit

In rooms transformed by argument the cracking walls return their early coats were white, with navy accents. Color tends to fit its age and so comes back. Burnt orange at the skyline, 1970 succeeding 1969 could not refrain from giving way. Like evening when downtown collects: familiar flights on strangers' faces, bedrooms seen up into from the street, a tide of blue light entertaining those now rich enough to live below 14th. The oldest word for window meant hemmed glow, that which can be passed or opened easily

Embarrassed by desires they invite, imagined things become predictable décor—the easy chairs and spider plants—through time, a giving forth of flashes. If the light green coils in the living room continue upward shape dissolves to fading rings reflecting hopes for equal pay. The next three years marched by no way to tell who painted them, but smoke above East River factories could look exactly like gray plants. The edges of a portrait touch the rest in time. Without its trucks, America would stop. They took him in

To custody, released him, told him to appear, adjourned for weeks the objects dance their bodies fully lent. My job: survive positions others equally compelled assign me. Emotions, weekend meals, their merger during holidays, examples of a tame expanse the face when undergoing strain responds with. How would a child endure a cubicle? Eventually like waves and flags each friendship with possessions ends inside five years another one drops out, a period effect, the public education plastics supervise. Intent on setting off

Forgetting, starting at the head, moves down. To medicate the stress of erranding, turn time into a temporary bed and fall across the city-colored canvas suddenly made sense. They run around asleep in fashion, correspond with friends inside machines, rhythms they're the same as. Going out of business signs I'm not the first addressed by, changes in the weather taking hold. Angry couriers, the summer's prices slash towards pleasant shocks they carry numbing agents for. In traffic lights permission hangs

Already headed into other scenes, but also moving through the mannequins of Bloomingdale's on 59ᵗʰ in 1981, a pronoun for I'm not sure what within the early life resists a scheme, maybe nothing. Chased around the room at night, the cars of conversation seeking refuge on tv, ideas become impossible to know as anything but raw materials added to a pulse. This power littleness possesses to entrance cuts through self-evidence. I'm saying for a moment lights are human

Crowds a face contributes surface to will let her reemerge towards emphasis by afternoon, removing tons of sediment. I called her "she" because she seemed legitimately gripped by certain choices made before her birth, i.e., there was no exit plan. Prose had found its way inside the room would overheat at night. By dinner I'd forgotten her in rituals where someone flew along a beam to take the seat of someone else. He thought of this as chasing lines that stop and turn

Left each morning slightly after eight, routine resettled dust in all the rooms before his key could hit the lock. But then I look outside and see the middle acts (in which they learn their fate) are done already ending now or winding down. The goal when traffic lights against increasing dusk present green holes becomes narration of the sales clerks headed home. Two horns go off to celebrate preemptively the accident avoided. Readying the house, he flicked the switch the light it throws

Inside the genre others are invited to what seemed at first the dreamy props now strangers they themselves turn out to be a party of. In Brooklyn marching with the PLP the cracks spread space through solids telling time. And fighting off the transitive neglect of those who hurrying in other circumstances press you undeniably you're lost. Transposed on errands through what look like ruins from above, the citizens secrete a mortar of intent, why bother following. With this in mind, a structure sent between

Fatigue and anger, vitamins, of being born at some remove from Sunday, leaving any world untouched, I guess I sing. But many other things show up. The safety of the ports, large gulls improperly inland, that rip within a point of sale; and lunch beforehand where we wondered whether forms detach from prior eras reappear as Morris Louis veils or if an accident is king of how museum shadows thicken into middle distances. Wrong to think of day as falling up and out of bed

Already angry at the offices, all matter is examples too annoy me; day replacing day projected out a rose-edge turns the nearest browns of circumstance, those rooms discreetly linked by easiness. You thought (as I do now) protected speech would be more musical yet common running through a series: courthouse steps. Which say, But help me with this flag, then stop right there with nothing else to offer. Fantasy: the crowd that gathers falling back still thinks

Peripheries stream by, the hair attempting to keep pace with aftershocks a modest laughter sends its way, a room supposedly beyond the windowsill, the head content within a neck's quite general song. Part nurse, part soldier, citizens protect the whole and so they fall in love with neighborhoods, with they allowed to mean all things and neighborhoods outlasting supersession, verging on the musical in overlapping rising voices from next door, the angers that have flocked

Together to examine each the other's fluttering edge, I used to tell myself this story: civics is a game of heads and tails removed. Then would fall asleep to prove it. Even drifting down the storefronts to a private square, I got concerned about her chances in a world where angry pipings cross without regard. Only snow machines can quiet them then only long enough resumption goes withstandable. Most thoughts confirm the season they occur in ends. The driver silently agreed

I'm not so sure I know why anybody pays the fare. We grew up in the 70s or 80s then some fractures rang. I won't eat anything capable of song and you, you've grown the short invisible lead that pulls you from an appetite. A lazy panic like the line I'm trying to remember loving quoting it for you: the flower absent from these men in evening coats are ice a step away from them espousing freely. To get citation right you'd have to read past everything but be

Someone other than the one who keeps the books, I use first person and the second tags along. You'd need to have the contracts long before your birth, be born on Sunday, translate living as the sentences that stopping on a dime go on. Do you recall how learning when alone felt much like leaving eastern states? The goal of reading prose was hold a stranger's gaze until its coins had shaken you then ran to mother in the other room, but swap in jail for goal and getting off the bus too late

For other room, replace the words with prose with everything a walk across the park at 86th could be, the sentence with unplanned parades dispersing slowly blocks forgotten habits take new forms. Who are these men the winter streets impose, quotations? Typically, I take the nearest public transit, ripped from unknown thoughts by trains arriving go on walking through the snow, remember, stop, turn back and yes, it's Lincoln Center. In falling right outside a lamppost's glare I lost what I went back for every seven days

The index crashed between the pillars of the week. You'll find a massive game of solitaire in progress underneath the window cops were laughing with the doorman in the dusk. I'm thinking of a statue going shopping in New York but stopping somewhere privately forgetting to perform. Each task contains this threat: you print the boarding pass invades the house. But he remembers holidays instead, decides to draw between all wounds a line when walking past the calendar, beginning with parked cars emitting outlines under snow

Where faces keep invisible they imitate one's own debris. Their project like
a flag in flight each winter headed south confused. The words emitted keep
improvisations half at bay. Even windows are to-do lists under ice. The idea
would be to document the way pedestrians perform a vandalism of attention's
properties. A word that once meant reuniting broken parts (an algebra),
then any restoration underway, now means Times Square cleaned up, risk
management. So what I thought to say united in

A stranger passing mannequins looks like the friends reflections overlapping
make of her. The fate of choruses: to be replaced by sounds of registers and
automatic weapons, littleness transacting with the ear. I'd only say that to a
man on sick leave lying down inside us, come back soon. One foot upon the
courthouse steps, they end within "the how the day went," spinning off in
girlish wonder over whether there are ways to move unnoticed while asleep. If
stone steps succeed then why not

Stay in bed the better part of days spent practicing the color changes trees to
accusations. The plaza's three performance halls are clad in travertine, calling
out to those who cross against the light. I wanted to retain the European
Starling's angry self-sufficiency (released in Central Park in 1890), streaked
and dotted streamlined beings multiple enough it seems beside the point to
measure. Wind at certain intersections often blows their song away in sagging
loops they make a comedy's

Indignant notes on territorial intent, I dedicate this early work to propositions overturned, branches blowing free of ice, my friends and any children they might have, the dogs allowed offleash in Oakland and Sunol. Here I start believing song describes the power line or patio that hosts it, minus any notions of terrain. Big forces migrate through the little games released into a populace: Three Strikes laws, missing children, ads in which the happy finish off each other's sentences

Seen from above the private life looks like a dot, but feels more like coordinated spheres. They stay related death releases them. Her voice both bored and low, detaining strangers temporarily, as on a bus at night. Walgreens bloom wherever looked for while we climb the flattened stairs. A kind of thunderous tinkling when you grip the parts you love respond. Thing makes an anagram of night comes back, unchanged. The time was any evening after work, the small one getting started though inclined

To fill the cracks with comedy I picked a navy corduroy in which I would appear before the judge; he had an antique pistol on his desk I played with while he married strangers. Project: in paragraphs of novel length proceed to summarize collective dreams. While walking past the brownstones where they're filming next year's seasonal ensemble I remember any speech would cause the doors to open windows on the upper floors stay shut. You'd have to live across the street to know how that one ends

In sentences of three to seven years' duration staring out I married glass in which I saw the others weren't free of problems they pursued. And almost like they walked together, how the midtown shoppers went about their business. I think of these pedestrians as orchestrations played on stationary bike, the ballet lessons of a class now anxious grains of light I live in California, lime trees rock doves hop around in, currant scones. The early years pink tags their vandals left behind on brick still visible. And looping back

She tests resistances by skating on the wrong side of the ice. I'm told this varnish can appear (at certain thicknesses) a shade of blue on colder days to think one's way among obliging subtleties because the project, built by those who've disappeared, is all about the cracks. Precipitation, late fees from utilities, the same as little knocks expecting welcome. Dreamt I was a guide through misremembered verses filled with living men who then were set ablaze, the thing they made enough of heat and light to read

By now the city parks sleep standing up in spring the drug of choice politeness. They trust their vigilance if one forgets about the redder portion of the spectrum, nearest branches absently arranged. Today I might prefer examining the wall without a break, I've given up the window waking had returned a public life. A note was wrapped around the brick. You're meant to hear as well as see what passing hours bring, that stress reactions in the feet of hurrying pedestrians resemble maps

Without the sound off, families televised distribute twice the information. Muted, they still glow with what the walk to work could look like if you drift off first. Ingenious that the face would capture both these processes, could swap in others, wake, and any anger hadn't disappeared. Yes, I'm saying friendship sleeps in even motivated speech, adjusting public shocks. A task: endure neglect from passersby but love the painting they compose unconsciously, my laugh the errands separating those who'd walked in step

Within surroundings so familiar, shorn of reasons why they wouldn't be, the walk flows private rivers past a lie of things, the Oakland docks, their disposition towards the sun. Why let horizon happen that consistently. If patterned ways of getting mad at pain that can't be felt directly fall within my scope now limited to trying anyway. Inaudible, the struggles of the grid, though blinking cursors almost have a sound. Basically my orders are I check the front door's locked and night's a country. Yes

Other worlds appear where monologue leaves off. Like saying I don't need you to your image in a film, embarrassing. The auditory still hallucinations haven't stopped yet where your speech is called for heard or hear potentials of a rhythm I insist can be revisited a second time. A stressful crossing, trees that don't survive indoors, apartments friends sublet to friends of friends, equivalent departures. That any time refers to any other's yesteryear meant also every three years could

Remind me of the lines I'd like to quote again? They manage both the crisis and responses varied, falling into three main groups. The city can resist no metaphor until the poor have left and that they never do. If even small disaster strikes I'll banish everything, respond without reacting (you can live downstairs), will walk beside you unobtrusively. In other words, you'll have the room you need to build an ugly laugh from hypotheticals denied. Insisting to the end they aren't old, this dream of pronouns

I can't use because the color runs. Against my better judgment thought to sing of preferences, inclining towards the floating bags that people carry on. Their distribution spells a sign my paranoia's justified the bus in stopping rhythmically at three block intervals determines us. I mean that from a window city life bears witness to the industry of bending joyful heads. Crowded in their giving up the hours pass inspection of containers at the ports, for now just one in twenty pulled

Over to the left misorchestrations, little shocks where two of them keep getting in each other's way, as though directed, while a third looks on amused. Looking back I am the third, awake but like a background thrives that hasn't happened yet. I speak to friends about the story they instead begin describing prices falling where they are, amazing verticalities the earth records in shifts to change the subject back. Years of this and you'll be muttering wet wind in coastal grasses always works no more than going to

A state it's only common sense to walk around in unaware my screaming wasn't music. Yet democracy demands the better part of managers, wishes disciplined retelling autumn depths of system degradation taking place. Her mirror-image turns to serve a customer arrives at facingness. From East to West much windier than yesterday sent fallen spinning through exchanges in the tunnel in the park, leaves disappearing waves a troubled sleep returns. The power of the screen is colored

Filters legendary for their alterations of a room, even gardens seem to boil seen through bars if moving past them. Not only can you now say nothing back to these transmissions, but then pride yourself on knowing they can't hear you still suspect the opposite as sun steals up the scaling of both thoughts. The show lasts thirty minutes of internal motions unpredictable as flame: a public's two dimensions projected through the glass. At first they talked beyond the surface of the screen

Through dimness not unlike a motor's blended sounds I'd dreamt Manet was wrong, there was a way to dodge the businessmen in crowds, but moving like this took more years than anyone expected, only happened there, and then I woke up certain I possessed somatic names in which real rest would be subsumed or sat content beyond reliable horizon. Cities are the better part of sleeplessness but misapplied is what I'd sing to daughters if I had them. Now awake

If modeled arborescently, but with the trunk removed, subway systems branch by color, serving some priorities as though there weren't others anymore. A car screams into life, just loud enough the sound moves overhead before it dies. A story of the minor supersessions any room could hold or open onto. Yes, I woke up wondering of series are their terms jackhammer sounds on 22nd for a year recurring ticks and flashes wave goodbye or is what came before less clear than that it did

No question, I should speak entirely in slashes. The plans still hovering above the power lines I didn't notice for the first three days. Now they come all the time in the world. Brief interviews don't capture falling through no space repeatedly forgiven yet ignored. Regarding those thick cables hosting current, I believe I hear them saying looking now no longer separable from running out while giving evidence. In other words, the family's plans extend throughout the week

A flight of steps absorbing sound within gray wells, one way winter laughter's been described. My project now to learn the French for still connected to a falling tomb of particles. I guess it's possible a people glides along from house to house as though a language made of equal signs, but haven't seen them. Life would melt in each attempt, torn again by action overseas. Ignoring horns and sirens, steam from manholes offers changing endwords, modern Provençal

For dizzily above the world the blinking lights, collective life in flight, abstractedly survive commemoration. Then the season turns and current flows into the picture. A muddy coat of brown gives way, revealing brilliant greens and blues about the earth there's little more to say unless you stop and listen to its roaring unawares. The lining sewn into the coat each spring removed in sympathy with green recovering between the redwoods. You'd expect this of the face were it not for how it looks, looks out

Imagining the depths across the way men smile a definition of these dual processes. Out then back, the difference in one's heading marked by shopping bags beneath the arm. The struggle's right, the method obsolete. I want to call them seasons mean the orange poppies on a median. Replacement marks a tragedy can be exchanged for frames in which one sees the colored lines unfurled avoid the center of the canvas. Though on screen it looks continuous the current pulses, flowing through the grid they make

Their marks, a stirring up of sleepless forces passing through each other slowing down. At least to nod a small acknowledgment would be enough if understandably they have no time to stop. The ride to work all motion is or rest, a rhythm laughing at the courthouse steps and motorists I think they're called, remains of groups. Something you can leave but later could return to, picket lines, a project based on images of workers' faces coming off their breaks. They walk around a chant embarrassing

To say we have the opportunity to meet an understatement. In case we do, I've practiced both the private languages. Yours sounds like stocks keep dropping widening a hole persists the slot the mail comes through. Unlike the language of recovery advising patience means withstand invasion, buried structures buckle time is quoting seasons in the marble's cracks. But these are dreams the institution counts on so please promise not to laugh despite the audience beginning to

Sleep now, while I and your clothed body talk insurance premiums. The rose has custody at night is how I misremember it. He said he wants to do away with wages but remains content to sit beside a stream recopying the pronoun all words sing of at their leftmost edge. How else could classes walk together underground. Laughing bitter cold the head begins to bob and now I'm only one of many children of an hour headed down the steps. The platform spreads below the dove

Gray steps lead down into the platform. An afternoon still all it takes white flight to leave the frame. And yet translation isn't supersession any more than thinking to depart a laughter's poetry. Or windows dead technology of ice. If living well means living twice I learned to watch required being silent while the face received a glow, tilted slightly up to catch blue planes. At night the quiet grew to either side divisions fell, a standard piece of period home video performed as life. If you divide a still

Image into colored dots from overhead they look like occupation histories, there and only there most people couldn't tell you why. But to an infant this would fall way down the list of possibilities restrict themselves. Including I can't say your need or finding where the skin ends isn't cracks but world. In other words, from 8 to 10 p.m. dramatic action buries purposes the narrative condones. Example: Luddites phrased their care for workers through the breaking of

Can't check to see if this is right. In English those three syllables refer to native peoples of the region though they may be used more generally. Moving through the dealers on the corner (summer dusk) I heard them calling me ("White Knight"). If situated near a fatal crossing heads absorb the well-defended language on the other side, while those who in their language often call the place a name not used by its inhabitants nonetheless transmit a common way

To display the image coat the screen with phosphor so the background disappears. You may have heard the song they use, which glows when struck mnemonically. A hum the child brings forth to draw a picture coming closer may produce a superstimulus, inviting and repelling equally. The cell phone camera through a window captures violence unprovoked so close that even bees are sometimes fooled. That's why he spent those years are over

Now, in exile, still responsible for not returning home, the standard days of every week, their order, name, and rank, the ledge on which the others rest when not in use, the time remaining falls like blood through quickly standing up to see. Truth and reconciliation minus truth leaves years I keep forgetting that I sent it to myself as backup, so when I see there's mail I get excited ways of making sure the work survives, its winter flight. Stand a few feet further off and you can't tell

An infant's face ignores the anthem is about some colored lights. Only experts should identify the sex of chicks, with ice and roads no way of telling yet. They branch too quickly, disappearing into shading off the curve of earth today was "very light and dark." I didn't know you couldn't marry mirror images nor ward them off, instead a day spent looking for new threats becomes them. Other quarters send reports the equal sign is doubled minuses when you

Stare at anything but walls and you'll be disappointed in your pay. A head, divided from both face and tail, discovers time expresses contents. Three days running I went back and had him do procedures, breaking seals inside the wound. You hear the stories patiently they stop outside experience. The vancomycin brings out giddiness, a body hosting opportunities to laugh. Then the blood fell and the marriage ended suddenly I felt the honeycomb explode in secret rites I will survive

Nostalgic visits back, that script which takes your body looking up through windows, living there fantastically behind them while the shades are drawn. A girl who gazes out where I once did still hasn't thought to let me in because of sirens, distant now. Fondness for locations has no rights. If looking down the street I'm startled wet black roses vanishing are only tail-ends of umbrellas shut away within a room the rain has stopped then shame on me. Like music shared, unless immortal no one owns a house

The rhythm will address foregoing most of variation's opportunities. Actually, they made the corner safe. You can't go back but you can visit laughter marks one route, dividing properties until the shaking indistinct from sympathy, attempting yet again to match your stride to hers. The light has changed like trains the current mayor's unafraid to take but no, he's still asleep beside the stream and she's upset at frankly flowing past perdurable locales, how spring each spring survives to come to nothing but

The ruins and their ornaments suggest they managed nearly every aspect of the early life. Visiting, one's struck by moods recovering lost facts—what not to do if someone handed you a torch, etc. The ritual is simple, dress the young and have them dance like flames, an iridescence of the male head made available to all. At first it sounds like muttering from suburbs these complaints the motor he kept running like a note left on the kitchen table makes. Though constant still a wish for abdications you yourself provide

These dots, which are called pixels. Like prose the scene will never move beyond a square of light. The winter lasted past the proper date—is there a word for that? And if I understand correctly then you're saying there's a day and night to do so, hurry up, the future perfect timing's everything. Just beyond the street another, dimmer street the curve of earth refused. In several years of these encounters understand the difference lighting makes

The uniforms look drab, next year's events should be outdoors. The beam would always land there in the courtyard just as evening falls among effects. Your shoulders broad if unaware they hang above your waist attracts me. During holidays you fly the partial match between them and the others, never getting proper views of that tradition. What marriage is to closets courthouse steps will also stand for; cracks in rituals official talk repaints, you almost feel control resuming bodiless by eye alone

Against the day you see a little way to steer. The residue will entertain a crowd at night becomes more vulnerable to imitation rallies. I prefer imagining the group disturbs necessities but then you see the major outlets piping parodies of sharing sense. Out to the seasonless edge then looping back, though fewer operate on Sundays. The coffee's better but the light insane, a fragrant dust like not returning calls. His worries over family, friends, and job the entries in a single book they read by motion lights, a time

Surrounded by my having stood and standing up again I prove myself
incapable of isolation from durée. For now the gains go private losses public,
change so small one period will let the next one tell. Or would if I had read
enough to know what caused the rolling blackouts they control with ease,
a rip like wings. I hear the next six months (or nine at most) might fill with
news each day the worst still yet to come, updated at the top of every hour.
She laughed I knew the term securities

At such an early age, better not to speak such words incapable of bearing
feelings they engender there by the corporate fountain I rested. Saying: where
there is doubt descent is easy but he who dreams while sleeping doesn't fall
that far. Translation: at a distance everything looks ready. Result: let's enjoy
ourselves as long as we hold PDAs. Flashing eyes coordinates a photograph
can't capture during courtship there's no need. Then rose when unexpectedly
in part they all returned

Their gifts betray no sense of knowledge, cruise the middle distance, stations
I can't be certain my laments go understood. Attempts to trace the comic back
along the rails to origins in wedding song and boredom often race against
themselves. The sound can travel up and down the coasts for miles the ice
plant grows, magenta and invasive. I'm asking that you let me go alone or
travel with without your leaving signs. The coin they found rubbed smooth
had borne a head held captive on one side

You see families out on Sunday, I see Christmas lights all year divided into ferries back and forth on shorter paths inside the week, pleasant when uncoupled from exposure to spring rains. I drive a hybrid forms of which are parody, the song that runs along the side attempting partial matches. Traffic has a mood that just beyond the door dies down. Left ajar, my mouth's first word the summer glow of unexpected cities driving west at night, the business loops

She spoke as though electric light had reached the shantytown, but who could blame her while she held the floor. It's dangerous, I said, and laughed at how a private language someone else would read had flourished in Aisle Four as we approached. Tikrit would mean "go limp behind the eyes" while sunset functioned like a broken phone. Forgetting we're three hours earlier, she left a message free from content thinking vagueness guarantees I'll call you back. Half-siblings sleep in mixed-use lofts, an almost daily battle

With the system fully grounded hit the switch if hum persists it means sealed chambers lie beneath your feet, you're at a podium, or speaking while awake. So this is Paris, gray and friendly, ancient city smells collected in the floating ironwork. Each plot may have a value of its own, beloved $x$, but contestation uses everything as currency. I guess the national chains expect to run their New York flagships at a loss. While ruins urge you reconstruct their ethos irretrievably you walk

Among the cypresses a breath expended won't return. So take the blanket's other end and fold it till you reach her side, the free one still available in trying times. If spending that much time before the screen is wrong, then add in daily walks, the "tourniquet effect" will let the blood back in. She argued they should file all documentaries within the horror genre while the water table drops. Exhausted after this, but not yet ready to give up, concerned she's right, but still opposing

Certain struggles I might have an answer to, taking breaks (as she advised) to stare and let the eyes adjust, and sleeping at the same time every night, concerned a dream I can't remember woke me up, all this the record skips the bridge collapsed. Without commercial breaks each episode can end the way the next one starts with shots. The horror section's somewhere in the back. Pronounced correctly words are chords but otherwise. Futures still entrapped by circumstance, the country moved to claim the land shelf ice retreats

Down to a few grey scales. Have you considered driving poles into the earth at intervals a form of writing that records the assets of New York? The artist thinks so, overrun by starlings. Cold-war project: establish interstates for moving ordnance through Nebraska's suddenly dispensable locales. My theory's that there's always been technology or that no human can refrain from using unfamiliar things. Your neck for one, and hollows. Introduced, they both refused to smile, producing strains

Of song the less we say the better part comes back without embarrassment. Steep drops along the trail like drinking air. My phone and keyboard always could adjust to darkness now they also laugh expectantly, the perfect pets to practice running with beyond the lows the next eight days and rain. It's hard to take Sonoma seriously. The spoken drives away while written thoughts remain, the difference being how one hums along. But I was never sure which ones were loan words

Sound like verdicts being passed on whether dead things live. Say nothing when there's nothing good to say the necessary changes being made me feel at home until a palm tree bored into the view. Invisible activities result in sourceless sounds the window brings. I bought two lamps to push back dark but couldn't see the clock from there, strange that bird both wakes and sleeps against the power to predict. And when in use I felt betrayed by chat technologies you leave without your signing off

On private life's small keys I played an unconvincing song. Games of here and there held little power over me. But moved to make a virtue of necessity I took the bus (the phones were dead) and sometimes flew (before the doors had fully opened) out, determined now however briefly to retry a quality of sound allowed a lingering on in frozen air. The light looked down on weakened ties, a public feeling made to hover overhead till someone noticed that

The dome cannot be pierced but looking at the sky you choose a yielding starting point out changing states. Invasion happens just like custody, you never know your status in the hearts of cloud-shaped men. They may have been an inspiration for the shopping bag or raw materials for same as yesterday ablaze. When transports have to do with how stuff works you want to share the sudden gain in expertise, embarrassing if she stays otherwise engaged in forms of listening distractedly

Surprised rough sketches grew around the pen, she said goodbye while hanging up. No wonder then I tend to think of chains as naked. Steadily polluted, catching sun, a kind of running pride that no one takes the credit for, the rivers on three sides announce these settlers chose their situation well. They took their turns with rhythm, humming unsuccessfully to ward off ice. At night the crust that forms becomes that night's responsibility. While two makes sense as three's divisor

Years would leave the conquests terms in series gone astray. Doomsday scenario: things go on as usual the end of March takes several days detained in separate rooms their stories didn't match. No one's sure if pigeons cock their heads in flight or care which ledge. A platform shakes, collective fear as duffel bag. A song alongside conversation goes French gray at collar turning purple-green then turning back. The speed at which a starling lands co-varies with the kind of food it's after

April weather held no lasting sign. That kind of ritual requires dimming lights
until approval channels through the glow. The opposite of May Day is this
Saturday from nine to nine. I'd liken it to living in a railroad flat together
breeds contempt (I knew you'd say) both parties were at fault. Out through
unrelated conversations, sequels observation can't help running off to see
them there, the outdoor diners laughing over densities the foliage becomes
towards nightfall


Sounds seem louder when dissevered from their source, while music springs
from failing words. A working theory: those I don't yet know would love me
if they knew what I'd been through, even sympathy that slowed them down
a touch in passing would suffice till office tensions magically resolve. Yet no
one dances sober anymore unless insane or gathering around the ice floe's
edge excitedly they jostle till the first of them falls in, a beat, the rest now
safely wondering


If you can read this then you owe your teachers thanks. I heard a voice begin
to do just that, rhyme prose with those across the room in drunkenness like
press assembled on the courthouse steps—you know you're being used but
nonetheless excited standing there around the hole, expedience I think they
call it without end. Being used a parody of freer offerings, so get thee hence
they do. If I can make it through the end of May I'll question everything you
mentioned now seems right. I didn't know adults could sing

Technologies of starless navigation, joy from out of nothing much, the whereabouts of documents without which entering the country will be difficult, all these remind me of your climbing out of tightened smiles. The child his body hid sang lines that rolled up dollar bills would double back on. I fell asleep withdrawing. Milieus, disguised, continue on across the dome implied by city lights. Meanwhile the face stays slashed within unseen professions jobs got easier to quit though often scarred I'd get another soon

The period in question strings of colored lights, embarrassing they've hung them up some time to come. I'm saying that in trying to become concise the year ends awkwardly. They gave each other gift certificates whose thefts concealed a darkness fell to make the room more private. I haven't learned the unmet form the most important group, still time to do so. Yet the writing looks unchanged throughout, betraying little sign of age, disease, or mood in which he could complete the irony. Alone, I worked all night walled up

To you I owe my recent fascination with the details of regimes. They have a unifying look a single day would hardly tolerate. Pink cactus flowers, Pontiac's demise, things the week contained. When done she'll spend more time with both of us admit we feel this way. Transliteration of their calls still not the same as hearing CNN announce returns then host reporters via hologram they're gone now. Nothing could prepare the crowd to hear his blend of rhythm and sobriety nor did they want to stand unmoved he sat there nodding

Off a ways one sees pedestrians committing to a path through other bodies opening and closing in the situation room. Squinting when the lights go on as if my eyes held wishes disappointed power didn't come from coal. Yes, waking up had always gone that way, struggles half-obscured in "blood and fire," yellow, red, and gold at cheek and throat. I turned the moment on his face was shining out of gratitude for aid, recording that effect successive waves return from just beyond the shore where ice rode free

Use of these motifs suggests a supple understanding that the face and head can turn repeatedly. The pattern of the shield was raised with spears like current hours sent through time to see, so some believe it written very quickly others soon agreed. The owl or spider hidden on the dollar bill rewarding paranoia is if anything a printer's mark. Viewed through small embedded lights, North Oakland looks like contests won by quiet whites and pinks the jasmine spills. No chance of living anywhere but testing grounds

Of marriage say they can't afford to win the fight continuing allows them new recruits. Eventually the steps outside sound indistinct from cracking ice or banging on a table, those demands. I went alone, accompanied. Unaware your eyes were closed, an exercise in trust, the euphemisms from that time (as though December needed any more) now look like ways live feeling deadened walking forward into crowds. No one spoke the contents in their bag of errands glowed

Until he couldn't take it, so disgusted by the holidays they'd broken down the Walmart's doors and trampled several children in a parody of getting back what's theirs. Damage both a measure and a measurement, they make their last attempt to settle down. Her mania begins with overspending, "gifts." Your wages went so far you try again it clogged. Surprising how remembering a private pain resembles car alarms. Walled towns and river bridges both gave way

Before a future no one lives to see arrives repent. Assembly lines: amusement parks for products riding belts through time is falling snow still coming down the white of shredded packaging. We watched together and apart a memory in other eyes revived. The argument went down some unrescinding paths he failed to see how leaving would improve. On finishing the class I feel used up the time we had but wouldn't want to vouch for their experience. Recent cuts

Both ways across the mouth goes breathing speech. Obesity was common on the graveyard shift I worked for several years then left like Bartleby. Afterwards I thought of as events quotations bring. So visits home were reading foreign text by dimming lights, the prep work done. She comes back in to join us, pleased we follow scripts. The sun revolves around the earth revolves around the sun. Looking at the waves I tried to be completely stationary, swells they used to call them. That New York is gone

Beneath prosperity an older country waits, but if full candor is your god the past looks wrong. If not, a kind of languor then at having limbs. This figure represents the English influence and holds a "sounding-lead." Between the crossed arms of the windmill beavers flanked by barrels stand for native products mentioning lament. The middle rests like policy—it's not the NYPD shield for nothing. Though sitting on the water where our thoughts assemble furniture it's hard to think of them as having done

Too much regarding sentencing reform is not enough. Avoiding summary, the prison dully glows with certain colors banned. Long before they run for local office they have trained to speak while looking through a window unaware of on which side the house is none can say. All alone the laws change helplessly we teach them anyway they're building more without consent, far off across the water undetected. The system runs on shock and modeled acquiescence like the dominance in packs of dogs. Looted, bombed, and burned

The snow is falling generally, a paraphrase. You're doing fine inside the claim you haven't seen the sun for several days as though my care could also disappear. The public works he promised sounded like a story told to children drop their toys in time. Softly this economy holds all who have it. A hand will not release its branch until the next one's grabbed he thought of trade beginning in those private moves. The next few weeks look hard for you like always

Already I had fallen into habits he objected to, quoting useless French, confusing series with the veils of Morris Louis, forgetting that in '66, and '80, and '05 the New York City transit workers struck. The problem with the summer work: an absence of demands that driving through the rain to get a toner cartridge doesn't satisfy despite the asphalt mirrors it unfurls along a street. The face confessing secrets minus speech will also coast, while music shared from peer to peer

The beaches overturn without a proper break. Holidays came quickly through this winter tiny lights climb up the side of into dark. Dissatisfied, I try imagining they turn out happy children somewhere summer far recessed. Pursue the implication further than the shade in drawing up I am invited, visiting and gone. Recradled, phones recharge the batteries at risk of half-life. Highways were a cold war project not for us the angry men transporting ordnance through the night

Lit up in flares the road makes here and there an orange glow, invasion optics spinning off on either side into the dark. When I was young I'd turn from reading to asleep forgetting I should mark the page. A parody of love, how insecurity of conquest guarantees a force remains were found for weeks within the rubble. Like a pronoun for the thought that stays outside, "come today in fetters to the marketplace," a bedroom usually. The hopeful names they give withdrawing services, clear skies

Cut back in sober press releases circular as quoting rounds, September never is the cold you feel comes from the past but let's accept they've got both houses now. Accommodation doubles as you can't please everyone. Technically asleep, old footage in new media awaits a check to see if inputs weaken after entering (they do). They lived as though they wanted to describe what motion was while I, because of native swiftness in the writing, held onto first results. The speed at which reception ebbs

In varying from coin to coin the profile turned to watch through time like melting ice. At first I thought the actors saw you too but had for any question useless answers, sort of like the handball courts on 91$^{st}$, being read to minus books. Now I think I shouldn't do much more than move between the table and the bed unmade, study carpet patterns for their makers' hopes. You see how easy, tempting even, while the rain rebounds off asphalt, to forget citation's glow

Stick with the work of being burdened by a figure stripped of ornament, the passage from and to the page, unpaid commutes. They speak like only death removes them from their rights but this too now debatable, the face as shield, connected to how oil does. A muttering comes forward changing on the way so when I say Con Ed you wouldn't hear refineries at night but surely think of them lit up as arrogance, at least admit they're in the world a speech transmits by reading lights

Visible behind the curtains partially obscured a sign supporting Proposition 8 next to a sleeping cat. Connection never was like rituals insist it still is bitterly I laughed, the joy at feeling what I thought, the room the farthest from the street. The bedroom twilight laden with the scent of vines I never knew the name of while in Stuyvesant. Rallying for stricter definitions Mormons managed to convince these idiots while those affected slept where bodies freely dedicate exchange

Is tragedy not permanently visited? What else could outcome mean the Prius swerved across the lane. Wisteria. To put it musically, before my birth I was a girl still unconcerned with her appearance hemmed in marching through the pass. I guess I'll draw comparisons across each other's strings the sunlight stored in cells. Who cares and yet how could you not, a wave machine. The impassivity in documentaries while watching lions take their young below

The bedroom window overlooked a loading zone. Three days of rain like nature coming back then gone, the same expected for tomorrow should be clear. Let it break over you, offer questions rather than determine her response. A silence after argument goes either way relieved the first shift's over. The rest is missing something goes there. Yes, I woke up several times went back to sleep, concerned with minimizing lines around the eyes complicit in their plans

For a house without an exit to the street was their conception of the body after death had grounded it. Twenty-five to life for almost nothing worked to free the hummingbird. Ready as the Taylor Law, he tracked the surfers patiently she watched their drifting right in loose relations never quite myself. I hoped my notes would compensate for lost experience pursues a smaller arc. All missiles daughters of a source unseen by victims hit. Dawn choruses suggest the same but musically. Admittedly these happen

In each other's world a current flows. Continuous as finite outline, overhearing how she practices relationships, you realize you yourself are little different on the phone. The laptops lie in different rooms nearby, a parody of love. It's very different in the prison, volleys shouting sounds recross a massive central well. A temple underneath another one, its function now reduced to yielding finds assistants make. Without an extra day that stops for no one, simple nods will have to do

What anti-litter ads convinced us of: pollution is consumers' fault, the native's tears produced by Dixie Cup. Ahead lie all tough choices while behind they're buried in foundation stones. The wise man calls in sick and spends the morning shopping for peripherals online. Our fisheye view in videos a home invasion made into the fantasy consumption speaks. Amazingly, receiving information from the past transmits itself throughout you manage not to copy ligatures. Did several fuses blow, no just the one

For now I kept on seeing ampersands, whose origin lies in the letters bound becoming none. A childish energy or that of nature's residents complained. Like photographs of coughs (the Schlieren method) sound remains invisible, the airflow lets a fired gun suggest that self-consuming nature of the noise the ears record. My theory that development takes place unevenly without a stable point from which to watch proved useless yet again. I wouldn't like to but am not particular

From space the ruins viewed up closer than we've come before the scale will jump around excitedly. Like saying that at night the ocean branches more, faint as the faint are here. Her dress suggests the problem with discrepant wages, their feathered varying. But you prefer to dance without the equity of witness. Most agree: the office will sustain unhappiness by laughing undetectably divided into shifts. I'll eat it if it has a face but doesn't growl or sing there is no difference

Commuters feel quite safe among while dominated by the fact of their reflections overlap. Though some I'm sure are glad to go through turnstiles others aren't ready yet, wearing faces primed to throw new sentences the second public language shifts. Surprised that someone hasn't hit the IRT or 4, 5, 6 already every cheek now glows with this potential's light consents and goes. Together in the car we form a friend's extended family without our knowing very well or how

To play this game my pertinence dissolves to bodies moving under heads without direction, social rivers. Seated in the popular equivalent of damaged thrones I'll guess each reason fluctuates. The rolling blackouts signify you can't tell night has fallen till you reemerge. Without a word for this persistent version of surprise though anger minus thoughts could grab the screen. Someday HR will shut it down from sheer embarrassment, the money shrugging while they laugh

No one's thinking of what's next, the rocket landing in the ocean ice bridge breaks that pinned the shelf behind it larger than Connecticut. Up and down the corridors I couldn't keep from telling them the voice's embers were a figure for how little of intent. Most workflow has this quality of parody, matching stride for stride the long descent to platforms crowded with a sea of bags. And each one really means a life among the others having done it to themselves. The protest song before it starts combines the other arts

When fired suddenly I fled the conversation hoping it would be pursued. If private languages exchange receiving imbricated sounds as though the hall itself were muttering they aren't satisfied. A colleague plays a friendly stranger unembarrassed by the hand that holds you both are falling bodiless without their noticing. From all the routes available take three at every meal, the rest abandoned after six the doors close automatically. I hear my steps like helpless rhythm made objections to a solitude

No different from my passing back and forth between two houses, when asleep I tend to lose the word for forms extending over time regained. The window onto 91st takes moments looking out requires swinging into view. She's angry at the edges of her hair all angles of request you're there before internal light attacks the screen. Returning to New York in waves anticipating futures underneath the French for earth in English sounds like rip, I walked on guiltily then made a show of stopping when I turned

Around this time their euphemism got a holiday. More willing to encounter perils when asleep, her hand extended absolution's parody. I stepped towards her full of speech without a plan I sidled forward more to enter the vicinity. Amazing how the courthouse steps will reappear at dawn the snow has melted to a faulty score, guilty of a crime like walking. Headed at a stranger thinking of him breaks the rules. The problem with acknowledging the midtown streaming men and women looks like if

Pursued alone a reading fails to meet the definition of technology. Swap in broken sleep or friendship and you have at best low hum. In static everything is moving so the whole thing looks quite still I can't just sit there every night without suspecting pattern will drop in. Now the broadcast day no longer ends, I call the feeling coming up from subways finding freezing rain determination. I like to think precipitation sponsors solidarity, at least a cheeriness at going through discomfort ill-prepared together, broken waves

The people fall in line like strings their "time past lights the time to come." Already possibilities ignored, they have no faith clean coal is really never cared about the consequences. Against that backdrop private language orders anything could count as captive advertising. The step increase in wages caused an envy they can measure now the microfeelings on a face. You feel like looking half as much but can't help acting part responsible a screaming comes across

The sky above the temple lets the earth become an earth, a sheaf of forces gathering. Distractions form a comedy I run through correspondence, many Tomahawks each day though some of them reminders ruins lit from underneath at night museums now. Awake, no difficulty muting anger seeps back in without your entering commands. I'm saying friends are fiber optics running underground. The false dawn choruses revisit ramifying in a straight line looping back across

Exuberance unthinkable if separate from a remedy, the thing becomes a meditative hum of doing dishes while not listening myself, that spaced-out while falling from terrainless vantage points. The door was off its hinges on this, the most important of elections. They think unflinchingly examining embarrassment must start with pieties about your origins then move on to present-day affairs, the world, in other words, but musically protracted. The project's less about content to be considered that

My friendship with fidelity renews itself as dailiness in waiting trains. I'm ready now to treat the smallest circle's implications, ants the rains bring in. In all directions optimistically imagined by pedestrians a pertinence dissolves, permitting new expenditures, especially for winter coats. The April days that disobey the season proves a tipping point approaches through the twilight now, but then I've never liked to make the bed. Let the messed-up sheets record a childishness retains its virtues when your hair goes gray

The resolution fails the further you zoom in, the street a smear of colored blocks. You'd have to be revolving lights to understand homecoming's charms. The walls stay mostly blank but that can be embarrassing as being judged by choices bravely made their home was always full of guests, citations of citations, mutual acknowledgment you don't both have to be there for. She planned to WWOOF her way across the country colors had divided states abstractedly

From any stranger's face the prose of errands shines potentially. Traffic lights off ice at night remind me of the sun in waves behind dark curtains drawing shut. The last five years or so I kept the power to refrain from saying otherwise. In falling back a habit grows like talking while asleep, invasion songs. The threshold melts, consulted faces sewn between transported and annoyed. I'm angry day announces rhythm's supersession and by day I mean in other words than this is it

Ends twice like houses does, humming with internal distances. The other worlds will also have to wait. Going there three times a week through living motives thinking they're not grasping mine, between invisible and visible no conflict resolution now you think you see. Inventing more efficient lights and volunteering, taking buses to the past and letting eyes warm up before their runs, you'd think he'd written every book or met the one who lay across the sexes like a bridge

Funding now requires private lives embrace catastrophe. The longer messages go left unanswered questions falling down inside a crowd. A trail reminded him of knotted scarves, their ending too familiarly inside the need for doubling back. And yet the edge possessions cut in air provokes a thought of more can be relied upon. 8th Ave is blocked but yes, whole neighborhoods can be revisited. Giving minus any thought of reciprocity a pronoun used if lost

The ability to breathe for several minutes while first person reigned. The sun revolves around the earth revolves around the sun. Why let horizon happen that consistently a shock the week returns with differences, he loves them both. The children of an hour fading out, they've done no ill except transmit their thoughts. A fantasy: instead of wiretapping citizens the country resurrects the party line then does away with phones entirely. Suspended in delays connecting flights produce, I thought both coasts

## ACKNOWLEDGMENTS

Grateful acknowledgment is made to the editors and staff of *A Public Space, Berkeley Poetry Review, The Boston Review, Columbia: A Journal of Literature and Art, Critical Quarterly* (UK), *Hand Held Editions, The Iowa Review, Lana Turner: A Journal of Poetry & Opinion, Maggy, No: A Journal of the Arts, The Offending Adam,* and *Perihelion,* where versions of these poems have appeared.

I'm indebted to Ben Lerner for reading everything before it was written; to my editors, Cal Bedient, Forrest Gander, Bob Hass, and Brenda Hillman for including this work in their curation; to Rachel Berchten and Madeleine Ward for their work on the interior and exterior of the book; to Jeff Clark, Cyrus Console, Timothy Donnelly, Graham Foust, Judith Goldman, and Joanna Picciotto for syllable-level attention and encouragement; and to the students and faculty of Berkeley, Iowa, and San Quentin for their thought and its refinements of mine.

NEW CALIFORNIA POETRY

| *edited by* | Robert Hass |
| | Calvin Bedient |
| | Brenda Hillman |
| | Forrest Gander |

*For,* by Carol Snow

*Enola Gay,* by Mark Levine

*Selected Poems,* by Fanny Howe

*Sleeping with the Dictionary,* by Harryette Mullen

*Commons,* by Myung Mi Kim

*The Guns and Flags Project,* by Geoffrey G. O'Brien

*Gone,* by Fanny Howe

*Why/Why Not,* by Martha Ronk

*A Carnage in the Lovetrees,* by Richard Greenfield

*The Seventy Prepositions,* by Carol Snow

*Not Even Then,* by Brian Blanchfield

*Facts for Visitors,* by Srikanth Reddy

*Weather Eye Open,* by Sarah Gridley

*Subject,* by Laura Mullen

*This Connection of Everyone with Lungs,* by Juliana Spahr

*The Totality for Kids,* by Joshua Clover

*The Wilds,* by Mark Levine

*text* 10/16 Electra  *display*  Eurostile Extended
*compositor*  BookMatters, Berkeley
*printer and binder*  Maple-Vail Book Manufacturing Group